Multicultural Meals

Bobbie Kalman

Crabtree Publishing Company

www.crabtreebooks.com

Created by Bobbie Kalman

For Susie and Helen, two exceptional multicultural cooks,
and Oskar, an uncultured, indiscriminating, relentlessly begging canine gourmand

Author and Editor-in-Chief
Bobbie Kalman

Editors
Kristina Lundblad
Kathryn Smithyman
Niki Walker
Rebecca Sjonger

Art director
Robert MacGregor

Computer design
Samantha Crabtree

Production coordinator
Heather Fitzpatrick

Production assistant
Katherine Kantor

Food preparation and recipe-testing
Kristina Lundblad
Valerie Martin

Special thanks to
Erika Olarte, Jennifer Olarte, Clara Godoy, Federico Olarte, Jayson Foster, Adrienne Foster, Aimee Lefebvre, Alissa Lefebvre, Amanda Lefebvre, Jacqueline Lefebvre, Sophie Izikson, Joan King, Jonathan King, Chantelle Styres, Alexis Gaddishaw, and Kristina Lundblad, who loves cooking and eating as much as I do!

Consultant
Valerie Martin, Registered Nutrition Consultant, International Organization of Nutrition Consultants

Photographs
All photographs by Bobbie Kalman except the following:
Marc Crabtree: Cover (top right on both back and front covers),
    pages 6 (top), 12, 13 (bottom), 17 (bottom), 29 (bottom)
Other images by Comstock and PhotoDisc

Illustrations
Barbara Bedell

Digital prepress
Embassy Graphics

Printer
Worzalla Publishing

Crabtree Publishing Company

www.crabtreebooks.com   1-800-387-7650

PMB 16A
350 Fifth Avenue
Suite 3308
New York, NY
10118

612 Welland Avenue
St. Catharines
Ontario
Canada
L2M 5V6

73 Lime Walk
Headington
Oxford
OX3 7AD
United Kingdom

Cataloging-in-Publication Data
Kalman, Bobbie.
    Multicultural meals / Bobbie Kalman.
        p. cm. -- (Kid power)
Includes index.
    ISBN 0-7787-1255-9 (RLB) -- ISBN 0-7787-1277-X (pbk.)
    1. Snack foods--Juvenile literature. 2. Cookery, International--Juvenile literature. [1. Snack foods. 2. Cookery, International.] I. Title. II. Series.
    TX740.K272 2003
    641.539--dc22
                                                        2003016196
                                                        LC

CONTENTS

MULTiCULTURAL MEALS

"Multicultural" means "of many cultures." In this cookbook you will find recipes from several countries and cultures around the world. Some of the recipes have been changed slightly to be more **nutritious** and to contain less fat, but they taste the same or similar to the original recipes.

Note: The children who appear in this book do not always represent the cultures from which the recipes come.

French bread and rye breads

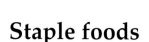

pita pocket

Staple foods

When preparing meals from different countries, **staple foods** play a large part. Different countries have different staple foods, depending on the type of crops they grow. Staple foods are foods that people eat every day or even several times a day. Many people around the world eat some form of bread each day. There are all kinds of breads—wheat bread, rye bread, French bread, white bread, and multi-grain bread—just to name a few. In some parts of the world, people eat flatbreads. **Pitas** and **tortillas** are examples of flatbreads.

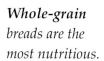

Whole-grain breads are the most nutritious.

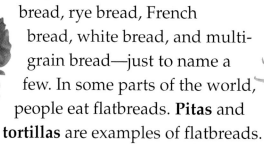

tortillas

4

Noodles, rice, and beans

In some countries, including China, Japan, and Thailand, people hardly ever eat bread. Instead, rice and different kinds of noodles, such as rice noodles, wheat noodles, and buckwheat noodles are the staple foods. The most nutritious noodles are made from whole grains. Italians eat both bread and noodles called **pasta**. There are hundreds of pasta shapes, each with many names.

In many countries, lentils or beans are eaten every day. Beans are often combined with rice or noodles to make meals even more nutritious. Together, they provide **proteins**, which help your body grow properly.

*Noodles come in many shapes and colors. The noodles on the right are Japanese **udon**, or buckwheat noodles.*

The spice of life

One of the reasons we enjoy eating foods from other countries is that they taste different. The different flavors come from the **herbs** and **spices** that are added to the dishes. Herbs and spices come from plants. In the past, cooks used whichever herbs and spices were available in their areas. As a result, certain herbs and spices became part of the traditional foods of various cultures. Garlic, for example, is used by people of most cultures. Italians and Greeks use herbs such as oregano, thyme, and basil. **South Asian** spices include curry and cumin. In China, Japan, and Thailand, people flavor their food with soy sauce, ginger, and lemon. In the **Middle East**, cinnamon, nutmeg, mint, and lemon play a big part in how dishes taste. Which are your favorite spices? Try the recipes in this book and discover some new and exciting taste sensations!

COOKING SAFELY

Cooking is fun, but it can also be dangerous if you are not careful. When you are using an oven, stove, knife, or food processor, make sure there is an adult in the kitchen with you. Accidents such as burns and cuts can happen quickly! **Allergies** are another common food-related problem. Before you start cooking, have an adult who knows your allergies check over each recipe's ingredients. Some **processed foods** may contain hidden ingredients such as nut oils. If you are allergic to nuts, carefully read the labels on foods such as dried fruits and seeds.

When working with the oven, make sure an adult is present— and always wear oven mitts.

More safety tips
• Before and after handling food, use detergent and water to wash all the surfaces on which you are working, such as cutting boards and counters.
• Then wash your hands. Always wash your hands with soap and warm water after handling eggs and raw meat. When washing up, include your palms, the backs of your hands, your fingertips and nails, and between your fingers. How long do you wash your hands? As you soap your hands, sing the Happy Birthday song. Do not stop soaping until you have finished the song. Then rinse with warm water.

• Be sure to wash any raw fruits or vegetables thoroughly before you cook or eat them. You need to wash fruits that you peel as well, such as oranges, lemons, and melons.
• Always wear oven mitts when you are putting food into or taking food out of the oven.
• Turn the handles of pots and pans away from the edge of the stove so you do not knock them accidentally and spill hot food on yourself or others.
• Always use caution while you are preparing food or cooking it!

COOKING TERMS

When preparing the recipes in this book, you may see some cooking **terms**, or words, that aren't familiar to you. The pictures shown here illustrate some of these terms. The recipes include metric measurements in brackets. The letter "l" stands for **liter**, and the letters "ml" mean **milliliter**. When you see the words **teaspoon** or **tablespoon** without metric amounts beside them, you can use an ordinary teaspoon or tablespoon from your kitchen. In fact, many of the ingredients in this book do not have to be measured exactly. We use terms such as **sprinkle**, **dash**, **drizzle**, **pinch**, and **handful**. When you see these words, you can use a bit more or less of an ingredient.

slice, chop, dice: *cut food into even pieces*

grate: *rub an ingredient against a grater*

sauté: *cook food in a little oil or water on medium heat*

simmer: *cook gently so food bubbles but does not boil*

whisk together: *blend well using a whisk or fork*

handful: *an amount that fits in your hand*

sprinkle: *scatter solid or liquid particles over food*

core: *remove the seeds and stem from fruit*

mince, press: *squeeze food such as garlic through a press*

grease: *rub a pan with oil or butter so food won't stick*

toothpick test: *check if food is cooked in the center*

drizzle: *allow liquid to flow in a thin stream*

VEGETABLE CURRY

Curries, or dishes flavored with curry powder, originated in South Asian countries such as India and Pakistan, but they are now widely enjoyed by people all over the world. Curry powder is a combination of many spices that includes cumin, coriander, red peppers, turmeric, and fenugreek. Curries taste and smell wonderful. They are as colorful as the lands where they originated. Many curries are meatless, but some contain meat. In India, they are often served over basmati rice, which has a delightful aroma!

For 4-6 servings, you need:
- 2 cups (500 ml) canned chickpeas or lentils
- 1 large onion, diced
- 1 teaspoon (5 ml) grated fresh or bottled gingerroot or ground ginger powder
- 2 garlic cloves, minced
- 1 teaspoon (5 ml) curry powder
- 1 tablespoon (15 ml) coconut oil, grapeseed oil, or butter
- 2 large well-ripened tomatoes, diced
- ½ cup (125 ml) carrots, chopped
- ½ cup (125 ml) green beans or cauliflower florets
- ½ cup (125 ml) water
- 1 tablespoon (15 ml) fresh parsley, chopped
- 2 tablespoons (30 ml) lemon juice
- a pinch of salt and pepper
- 3 cups (750 ml) cooked basmati rice (see cooking directions below left)

curry powder

chickpeas

tomatoes

onions

garlic

lemon juice

carrots

parsley

gingerroot

How to cook rice
Rinse a cup (250 ml) of rice well in a colander and put it into a cooking pot. Add 2 cups (500 ml) of water, a tablespoon (15 ml) of coconut oil or butter, and a teaspoon (5 ml) of salt. Bring to a boil, turn the heat down to low, and put a lid on the pot. Cook the rice for about 20 minutes, or until all the water is gone. Fluff the rice with a fork.

1 Drain the chickpeas and rinse them under cold water until the water runs clear and is no longer foamy. Rinsing the chickpeas will prevent digestive discomfort.

2 In a large pot, sauté the diced onion, ginger, garlic, and curry powder in butter or oil until the onion is soft.

3 Add the tomatoes and keep stirring quickly until the mixture looks like a sauce.

4 Add the chickpeas or lentils, carrots, green beans or cauliflower, and water. Simmer for 20 minutes at medium heat until the fresh vegetables have softened but are not mushy.

5 Add the parsley, lemon juice, and a pinch of salt and pepper to the curry. Cook for another 5 minutes.

6 Serve your curry with hot rice. You can put the curry over the rice, as on the plate above, or serve it separately on a colorful platter, shown left.

PITA TOPPERS

A pita is a flatbread that sometimes has a pocket. It is a traditional food in countries such as Greece, Israel, Lebanon, Iran, and Iraq. A pocketless pita is similar to an Italian pizza crust. You can use pocketless pitas to create a variety of snacks, such as those shown below and opposite. Try them all! The recipe on this page is a delicious dip or spread called **hummus**.

To make hummus, you need:
- 1 cup (250 ml) canned chickpeas, rinsed and drained (see page 8)
- 2 tablespoons (30 ml) tahini (sesame paste)
- ½ cup (125 ml) water
- 1 tablespoon (15 ml) lemon juice
- 2 tablespoons (30 ml) olive oil
- 1 small clove of garlic, minced
- a handful of fresh parsley, chopped
- ½ teaspoon (2.5 ml) salt
- ½ teaspoon (2.5 ml) cumin
- a sprinkle of paprika

1 Place the chickpeas, tahini, water, lemon juice, one tablespoon of the oil, garlic, parsley, salt, and cumin in a food processor. Blend until the mixture is smooth.

3 To serve the hummus, drizzle with the rest of the olive oil and sprinkle paprika over it. Use the hummus to spread on pitas or as a dip for pepper slices or other fresh vegetables.

2 Slice a few pita breads into wedges and cut some peppers into slices for serving.

Pita Pizzas

You can make many kinds of pizzas using pocketless pitas. Each pita pizza is baked in a preheated 400°F (200°C) oven for about 10-12 minutes. Be creative and invent your own multicultural pizzas. Here are some ideas to get you started.

To make an Italian-style pizza, brush the pita with olive oil and put some tomatoes and olives on it. **Garnish** with parsley. Add grated mozzarella cheese if you wish. Bake and enjoy!

For a Greek-style pizza, brush your pita with olive oil and add spinach leaves, tomatoes, red onions, **feta** cheese, and black olives. Yum!

To make a Mexican-style pizza, start with slices of red onion and red and green pepper. Sprinkle with some grated Monterey Jack cheese and chili powder.

For a German-style pizza, core and slice some apples and arrange them on a pita. Sprinkle the pizza with raisins and cinnamon and drizzle honey over it.

What kind of pizza will you make?

11

GREEK SALAD

It is good to eat some raw fruits and vegetables every day because raw foods give your body important **enzymes**. Some enzymes help your body break down foods and keep your **digestive tract** healthy. Eating a salad each day is a good way to get enzymes. The two salads shown on these pages taste great. Try them both!

leaf lettuce

cherry tomatoes

For 4-6 servings, you need:
- a head of lettuce (romaine or leaf)
- 1 or 2 chopped tomatoes or 15-20 cherry or grape tomatoes
- about 1 cup (250 ml) crumbled feta cheese
- ¼ red onion, sliced
- 10-15 Greek olives with pits or ½ cup (125 ml) chopped, pitted black olives
- ½ lemon
- 2 tablespoons (30 ml) olive oil
- a sprinkle of oregano (optional)

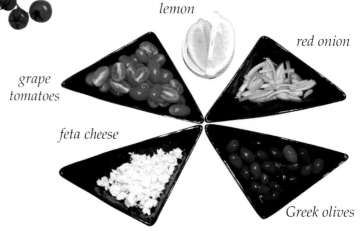
lemon
red onion
grape tomatoes
feta cheese
Greek olives

1 Wash and dry the lettuce leaves carefully and tear them into bite-sized pieces. Put them into a salad bowl.

2 Chop regular tomatoes into chunks or cut cherry or grape tomatoes in half. Spread them over the lettuce.

3 Crumble the feta cheese between your fingers. Add it to the salad.

4 Add the onion slices and olives. Drizzle the olive oil and lemon juice over the salad. As you drizzle, move your hand around to cover every part. Sprinkle on a little oregano, if you wish.

BOCCONCINI SALAD

Bocconcini is a favorite Italian salad named after the cheese from which it is made. Bocconcini is a soft, mozzarella-type cheese. It has a mild taste and looks like a boiled egg. It is especially good with fresh tomatoes and basil. Basil is a leafy herb. A squeeze of lime or lemon and a drizzle of olive oil makes this salad healthy and heavenly!

For one serving, you need:
- 1 tomato
- 2 bocconcini balls
- 1 lemon or lime wedge
- 1 teaspoon of olive oil
- a few basil leaves

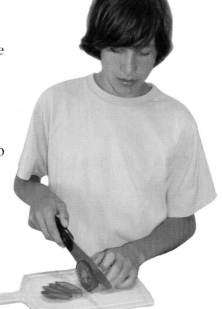

1 Cut a tomato into even slices. Then cut the bocconcini balls into slices of the same thickness.

2 Arrange the cheese and tomato slices on a plate in an artistic way.

3 Squeeze the juice of a quarter of a lemon or lime on the tomatoes and cheese. Drizzle on the olive oil.

4 Add some basil leaves. You can grow your own basil in a pot in your kitchen.

iTALiAN PASTA BAR

Pasta bars are a lot of fun because you get to choose your favorite pasta, toppings, and flavors. Start with a bowl of pasta, add sauce—or not—and then finish with the toppings suggested. There are over 600 kinds of pasta with more than 2000 names! Some are shown below. If you like your pastas colorful and nutritious, choose some vegetable pastas and mix in some of the whole-wheat variety. Be careful about mixing shapes because the thicker pastas will need more cooking time. Whichever pasta you choose, you can create a wonderful meal suited to your own taste.

To make 2 servings of pasta, you need:
- 2 cups (500 ml) cooked pasta (any kind)
- 1 teaspoon (5 ml) oil
- 1 teaspoon (5 ml) salt

Cooked toppings:
- 1 cup (250 ml) tomatoes, chopped, or grape tomatoes cut in half
- 1 cup (250 ml) mushrooms, sliced
- ½ cup (125 ml) onions, chopped
- 2 cups (500 ml) baby spinach, rinsed well
- 1 cup (250 ml) green peppers, sliced

Uncooked toppings:
- ½ cup (125 ml) grated cheese
- a sprinkle of parmesan cheese
- a sprinkle of red pepper flakes
- a handful of fresh parsley, chopped
- a handful of green or black olives

Optional ingredients:
- sauce
- meatballs

fettuccine

tagliatelle

cellentani

conchiglie

farfalle

spaghetti

vegetable and whole-wheat fusilli

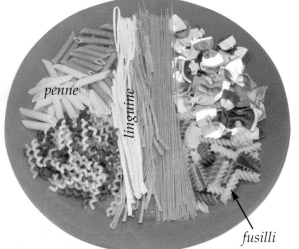

penne

linguine

fusilli

1. Put the oil and salt in the water in which you are cooking the pasta. Cook dry pasta for about 12 minutes. If you are using fresh pasta, cook it for only 2-3 minutes. Test the pasta by scooping out a piece with a slotted spoon, running cold water on it, and tasting it. If it is soft but a little chewy, it is done. With the help of an adult, drain off the hot water and rinse the pasta under warm running water. Put the drained pasta back into the pot or into a bowl.

3 To make your pasta dish, spoon about a cup of cooked pasta into a soup or pasta bowl. If you want to make a sauce, follow the recipe below left. Put your favorite toppings over the sauce or use the toppings without sauce. You can add the meatballs to any of the toppings. All the combinations taste great!

grated cheese

peppers

spinach

tomatoes

pepper flakes

mushrooms

onions

2 Sauté the tomatoes, mushrooms, onions, spinach, and green peppers separately and put them into bowls, as shown on the right. Also put the uncooked ingredients into separate bowls.

fusilli with veggie toppings

spaghetti with tomato sauce and meatballs

Tomato sauce (4 servings)
- 1 small onion, diced
- 1 garlic clove, minced
- about a teaspoon of olive oil
- 1 cup (250 ml) canned crushed tomatoes
- a handful of fresh parsley, chopped

In a saucepan over medium heat, sauté the onion and garlic in the oil. Add the crushed tomatoes. Let the sauce simmer for about 20 minutes and then add the parsley.

Meatballs
If you want to add meatballs, follow the recipe on page 12. You can use ground lamb or other ground meat such as turkey, chicken, pork, or beef to make this recipe.

BAGELS AND LOX

The word "lox" comes from a German word "*lachs*," which means salmon. The lox in our recipe is smoked salmon. Smoked salmon is a multicultural food that is enjoyed by people of many backgrounds. **Scandinavians**, or people from northern Europe, put it on rye crackers. Jewish Americans enjoy it on bagels spread with cream cheese, an open-faced sandwich that has become a favorite all over North America. It tastes especially good with lemon, red onion rings, **capers**, and **dill**. Capers are pickled flower buds, and dill is an herb with feathery leaves. To make this meal even more multicultural, use tortillas instead of bagels (see next page).

For 4 servings, you need:
- 2 sliced whole-wheat bagels
- 2 tablespoons (30 ml) low-fat cream cheese
- about 12 smoked-salmon slices
- fresh dill
- capers
- red onion rings
- a half lemon

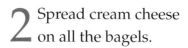

1 Buy pre-cut bagels, if possible, or have an adult slice them (they can be tricky to cut). Toast the bagel halves, if you wish.

2 Spread cream cheese on all the bagels.

3 Top each one with about three slices of smoked salmon.

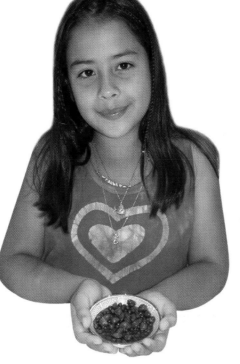

4 Add as much dill, capers, and red onion as you like. Squeeze some lemon juice over the salmon.

The capers and lemon will wake up your taste buds! They make this sandwich taste really good!

LOX ROLL-UPS

To make lox roll-ups, use the same ingredients as on page 18 but replace the bagels with whole-wheat tortillas.

1 Spread the cream cheese on the tortillas.

2 Put on the smoked salmon, dill, capers, and onions. Don't forget to squeeze on some lemon!

3 Carefully roll up the tortillas and then cut them into bite-sized pieces.

4 Secure each piece with a toothpick to stop it from unrolling. You'll love this delicious snack!

19

SPINACH QUICHE FROM FRANCE

Quiche is a pie from France that has become a favorite North American meal. It is easy to make, especially if you buy a ready-made pie crust. Quiche makes a great breakfast or lunch because it contains milk, eggs, and vegetables and will keep you from being hungry for a long time!

For a 6-slice quiche, you need:
- one 9-inch (23 cm), deep-dish pie crust
- 1 tablespoon (15 ml) cooking oil
- 1 small onion, diced
- 1 package (about 10 ounces/284 grams) frozen, chopped spinach, thawed
- ¼ teaspoon (1 ml) salt
- ¼ teaspoon (1 ml) ground black pepper
- ¾ cup (185 ml) low-fat milk
- 3 eggs
- a sprinkle of nutmeg (optional)
- ½ cup (125 ml) shredded cheese (your choice)
- 1 slice of precooked bacon, chopped (optional)

1 Preheat the oven to 400°F (200°C). Prick the pie crust with a fork so that it does not bubble while baking. Put it into the oven. When the crust is golden brown, it is done (about 10-12 minutes). Remove the crust from the oven to allow it to cool. Lower the oven temperature to 375°F (190°C).

oil · onions · eggs · cheese · salt · milk · pepper · spinach

3 In a mixing bowl, whisk together the milk, eggs, and nutmeg.

2 While the crust is baking, sauté the onions in the oil over medium heat for about 5 minutes. Over the sink, squeeze the excess water out of the spinach and then add the spinach to the pan. Sprinkle on the salt and pepper and stir.

4 Spread the spinach and onion mixture evenly on the bottom of the pie crust.

5 Sprinkle the cheese over the spinach and onion.

6 Pour the milk mixture over the quiche. If you'd like, sprinkle pieces of precooked bacon on top.

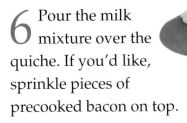

7 Place the prepared quiche on a cookie sheet and bake it for 35-40 minutes. Then do a toothpick test. When the toothpick comes out clean, the quiche is done. Take it out of the oven and let it cool 5-10 minutes before serving.

8 Cut the quiche into 6 slices.

9 For a complete meal, add a salad.

For a quiche that is much lower in fat, make it without a crust and bake it in a greased dish. It tastes great, too.

21

CHINESE LEMON CHICKEN

For 6-8 servings, you need:
- 4 boneless, skinless chicken breasts
- 1 tablespoon (15 ml) cooking oil
- a sprinkle of paprika
- a sprinkle of salt

For the cooking sauce:
- the zest and juice of one lemon
- 1 garlic clove, minced
- 1 tablespoon (15 ml) fresh cilantro, chopped
- 2 tablespoons (30 ml) honey
- ½ cup (125 ml) water

This favorite Chinese dish will have you smiling! The chicken is usually fried, but we have made a healthy version that will tickle your taste buds. It is sweet, sour, and tangy at the same time. We guarantee that it will be one of your favorites!

1 Preheat the oven to 375°F (190°C). Wash a whole lemon. Using a grater, grate its peel. This grated peel is called **zest**. When you have grated all the zest from the lemon, cut the lemon in half and squeeze the juice into a bowl.

2 Add the lemon zest, minced garlic, cilantro, honey, and water to the lemon juice. Mix well.

3 Spread the oil over the bottom of a baking dish and place the chicken on top. Sprinkle paprika and salt on the chicken. Pour the sauce over the chicken.

4 Cover the baking dish with foil and bake for 15 minutes. Take the foil off and turn over the chicken breasts. Bake for another 20 minutes, uncovered.

5 Put the chicken breasts on a plate while you make the sweet-and-sour sauce recipe, shown above right.

6 Serve the lemon chicken with rice and some steamed vegetables. Pour the sweet-and-sour sauce on top and garnish with lemon slices.

Sweet-and-sour sauce:
- the leftover baking sauce
- 2 teaspoons (10 ml) cornstarch
- 1 tablespoon (15 ml) bottled lemon curd or marmalade
- ¼ cup (62 ml) cold water

To make a tasty sauce to serve over your chicken, pour the sauce from the baking dish into a saucepan. Heat it at medium temperature. In a small bowl, mix the cornstarch and the cold water. Add the dissolved cornstarch and water to the pot and bring the sauce to a boil, stirring constantly. The cornstarch will thicken the sauce. To make the sauce sweeter, add a spoonful of marmalade or lemon curd. You'll love the great taste!

If you want to eat the chicken with chopsticks, cut it into slices you can pick up easily. To make easy-to-use chopsticks, place a wad of paper between the top ends of two chopsticks. Wrap a rubber band above the paper and another below it, as shown in the pictures.

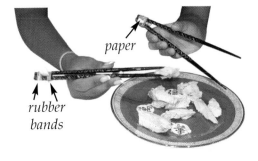

paper

rubber bands

23

THAI COCONUT SOUP AND NOODLES

This wonderful soup is typical of Thailand, a country in **Southeast Asia**. Traditional Thai flavors include coconut, peanuts, ginger, garlic, and spicy peppers. The food is so flavorful! When you try this soup, you will agree. We are sure you will become a Thai-food fan.

For 4-6 servings, you need:
- 1 onion, diced
- 1 cup (250 ml) mushrooms, sliced
- 1 cup (250 ml) cooked chicken, sliced
- 3 cups (750 ml) chicken or vegetable stock (broth)
- 1 garlic clove, minced
- 1 teaspoon (5 ml) fresh gingerroot, grated
- ½ teaspoon (2.5 ml) cumin or curry powder
- 1 cup (250 ml) canned unsweetened coconut milk
- 2 teaspoons (10 ml) fresh lemon or lime juice
- a dash of salt
- a dash of paprika or red pepper flakes (optional)
- a leaf of basil, cilantro, or parsley

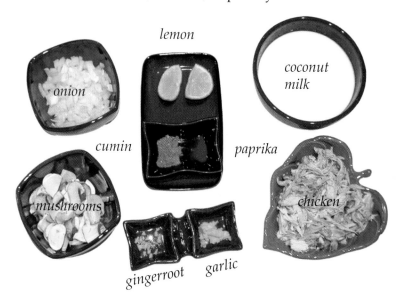

lemon

coconut milk

onion

cumin

paprika

mushrooms

chicken

gingerroot garlic

1 Dice the onion, slice the mushrooms, and cut or tear the chicken into small, bite-sized pieces.

2 In a saucepan, heat the stock on medium heat until it boils. You can buy ready-made stock in cans.

chicken stock

3 Add the onion, mushrooms, chicken, garlic, gingerroot, and cumin or curry powder. Simmer on low-to-medium heat for 20 minutes.

gingerroot

garlic

4 Add the coconut milk and stir.

5 Add the lemon or lime juice and a dash of salt, and your soup is ready.

6 Serve the soup warm. Make sure everyone gets some chicken and mushrooms in his or her bowl. Sprinkle some paprika or red pepper flakes on each serving and garnish with a basil, cilantro, or parsley leaf.

To make a favorite Vietnamese, Chinese, or Japanese meal of noodles and soup, put some cooked wheat, buckwheat, or rice noodles into a bowl, almost filling it. Pour some of the coconut soup over the noodles. Add chopped celery, green onions, and cooked shrimp (optional).

Enjoy your yummy noodle bowl.

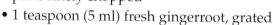

JAPANESE TOFU STEAKS

Tofu is a food made of soybeans. It is a great source of protein and **calcium**. It has very little taste on its own, but it can be absolutely delicious when it is cooked with other flavors. This Japanese tofu dish tastes great! The tofu steaks can be eaten on their own, chopped up and added to soups, enjoyed with rice and vegetables, or used to make sandwiches. Try them—you'll love them!

For 4 servings you need:
- 1 package of extra-firm tofu
- 1 spring (green) onion, both its white and green parts finely chopped
- 1 teaspoon (5 ml) fresh gingerroot, grated
- 3 tablespoons (45 ml) soy or tamari sauce
- 1 teaspoon (5 ml) sesame oil
- 2 tablespoons (30 ml) rice vinegar or other type of vinegar
- 1 garlic clove, minced
- 1 tablespoon (15 ml) cooking oil

1 Rinse the tofu block under running water.

spring onion

soy sauce

sesame oil

gingerroot

garlic

or tamari sauce

cooking oil

vinegar

3 Chop the onion. Peel and grate the gingerroot, making sure your fingers do not touch the sharp grater edges.

2 Cut the tofu into half-inch- (1-cm-) thick slices.

4 In a small bowl, prepare a **marinade** by mixing the onion, ginger, soy or tamari sauce, sesame oil, vinegar, and garlic.

5 Place the tofu steaks on a large plate. Spoon some marinade on each one.

6 Leave for 15 minutes, then turn the tofu pieces over with a spatula, as shown below, to soak the other sides for another 15 minutes. While the tofu is soaking in the marinade, preheat the oven to 350°F (175°C).

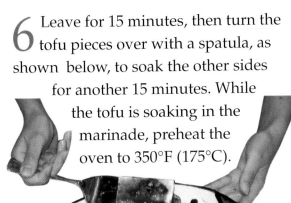

7 Spread the oil on a baking dish or cookie sheet and place the tofu on top.

8 Bake for 20 minutes. Turn the steaks over using a spatula. Bake for another 15 minutes or until they are golden brown.

9 Serve the tofu hot with rice or cold in a salad. Add a dash of soy sauce for extra flavor, if you wish.

Tofu steaks and fresh veggies make a delicious snack. Cut one into strips and try eating it with chopsticks!

27

MEXICAN FAJITAS

Not only is this Mexican meal colorful and very tasty, it is also fun to eat because you can create each **fajita** to please your own taste buds. A fajita is a tortilla that contains a variety of fillings. In restaurants, the meat, onions, and peppers used in this dish are usually brought to your table sizzling in a frying pan, but we have made a safer version for you to try. We promise that it tastes just as yummy! You can buy tortillas in any supermarket.

For 4 servings you need:
- 2 cups (500 ml) peppers, sliced
- 1 cup (250 ml) red onion, sliced
- 1 tablespoon (15 ml) vegetable oil
- 2 large boneless, skinless chicken breasts
- a sprinkle of paprika
- 4-8 whole-wheat tortillas

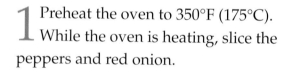

Toppings:
- shredded cheese
- sour cream
- bottled salsa
- guacamole
- assorted veggies (celery sticks, tomatoes, lettuce leaves, and onions)

1 Preheat the oven to 350°F (175°C). While the oven is heating, slice the peppers and red onion.

2 Spread the oil on the bottom of a baking dish. Lay the chicken breasts on top and sprinkle them with paprika.

3 Put the peppers and onions over the chicken. Cover the baking dish with foil. Bake for 30 minutes. Take the foil off and bake for another 10-15 minutes.

4 Take the chicken out of the oven and test a piece to make sure it is cooked through. If it is no longer pink inside, it is done. Once the chicken has cooled a bit, slice it into thin strips.

6 Arrange some chicken, pepper, a̶ on a tortilla. Top your fajita with s̶ salsa, veggies, cheese, and guacamole. To m̶ guacamole, mash an avocado, add the juice of ha̶ lemon and a sprinkle of cumin or chili powder.

tomatoes *celery and peppers*

guacamole

salsa

sour cream *onions*

5 After you have taken the chicken out of the oven, turn off the oven. To warm the tortillas, wrap them in foil and heat them for 10 minutes in the still-warm oven.

7 To eat your fajita, fold up the bottom of the tortilla and then fold the two sides toward the center.

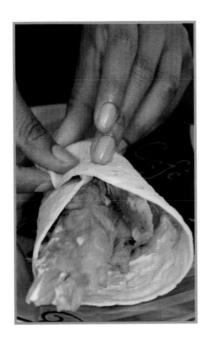

A COLOMBIAN FEAST

Colombia is a country in South America. This traditional meal from the region of Paisa in Colombia offers something for everyone. It is called *Bandeja Paisa*, which means "tray from Paisa." It does not take long to make and looks beautiful when served. The dish is served on a big oval tray, and each part is sampled by those sharing the meal. It serves 4-6 people.

Rice

Cook 1 cup (250 ml) rice with 2 cups (500 ml) water, a dash of salt, and a teaspoon (5 ml) oil or butter. (See page 8 for how to cook rice.)

To make the whole meal, you need:
- 3 cups (750 ml) cooked long-grain rice
- water (see rice and beans sections for amounts)
- 1-2 tablespoons (15-30 ml) olive oil
- 1-2 grilling steaks (or chicken breasts)
- salt, garlic salt, and pepper to taste
- one 19 fluid-ounce (526 ml) can of kidney beans
- 1 onion, diced
- 1 tomato, diced
- 1-2 avocados
- 1 package of corn tortillas
- 2 plantains

Steak

Ask an adult to help you grill the steak or chicken over medium-high heat until it is done. Season it with salt and pepper and slice it into strips.

Beans

1) Pour the beans into a colander. Rinse and drain them. Place them in a small pot with about ½ cup (125 ml) of water. Set aside.
2) Heat 1 tablespoon (15 ml) of oil in a pan. Add the diced onions and tomatoes and cook until the onions have started to brown.
3) Over medium heat, bring the beans to a boil, stirring often. Add the cooked onions and tomatoes and mix well. Season the bean mixture with salt or garlic salt.
4) Simmer the beans over low heat while the rest of the meal is being prepared.

Avocado

Just before the meal is served, cut the avocado down the middle and remove the pit. Sprinkle the avocado with lemon juice so it will keep from going brown. To serve, use a spoon and scoop a little bit onto each plate.

Plantains

Plantains are like big bananas but, unlike bananas, they need to be cooked. Peel the plantains and cut them into chunks, as shown above. **Score**, or make shallow cuts, in the pieces with a knife. Grill the plantains or fry them in 1 tablespoon (15 ml) of oil until they are lightly golden brown, turning the pieces occasionally. If you want the plantains to cook more quickly, remove them from the pan or grill using tongs and flatten them with the bottom of a cup. Return them to the pan or grill and cook them a little longer.

rice

plantains

tortillas

beans

avocados

steak

Tortillas

Right before you eat, heat the tortillas in the microwave for a minute or wrap them in foil and heat them on low heat in the oven for about ten minutes. Add the tortillas to the platter.

Share the meal with family or friends. Each person puts a little of each food on his or her plate.

GLOSSARY

Note: Boldfaced words that have been defined in the book may not appear in the glossary. (See page 7 for cooking terms.)

allergy The body's negative reaction to certain foods

calcium A mineral found in milk products, soy, almonds, and many vegetables, which is essential in building strong bones and teeth

digestive tract The tube and organs through which food passes to be broken down into substances that the body can use and wastes that are eliminated

enzymes Substances found in raw vegetables and fruits that act as helpers in the body to break down food, fight off diseases, and speed up healing

feta A crumbly cheese made from sheep or goat's milk and preserved in a salty liquid

garnish To make food look and taste better by adding a food decoration such as parsley

herb The leafy parts of an aromatic fresh or dried plant that is used to flavor food or to make medicine

marinade A liquid or paste in which food is soaked for a period of time for the purpose of giving it extra flavor

Mediterranean Describing the lands, peoples, and foods from the countries surrounding the Mediterranean Sea

Middle East The region that includes Egypt, the Arabian Peninsula, Israel, Jordan, Lebanon, Syria, Turkey, Iran, and Iraq

nutritious Describing foods that give the body energy and help it grow and heal

pasta A noodle-like food from Italy

processed foods Foods to which sugar, color, fat, or other chemicals have been added

protein A substance found in meat, milk products, soy, beans, and many nuts, which is essential to the body

South Asia A region that includes India, Pakistan, Nepal, Bhutan, Bangladesh, and Sri Lanka

Southeast Asia A region that includes Thailand, Vietnam, the Philippines, and other countries

spice Ground-up parts of plants, such as roots and bark, used to flavor foods

whole grains Grains that have not had their nutritious parts removed

INDEX

3 1333 03309 9951

1 2 3 4 5 6 7 8 9 0 Printed in the U.S.A. 3 2 1 0 9 8 7 6 5 4